TAE KWON-DO

White Belt to Yellow Belt

**The Official Tae Kwon-do Association
of Great Britain Training Manual**

Produced by the Senior Instructors of the TAGB

A & C Black · London

First published 1995 by
A & C Black Publishers Ltd
37 Soho Square, London, W1D 3QZ
www.acblack.com

Reprinted 1997, 1999, 2000, 2001, 2003

ISBN 0 7136 4104 5

A CIP catalogue record for this book
is available from the British Library.

Note

Whilst every effort has been made
to ensure that the content of this book
is as technically accurate as possible,
neither the author nor the publishers
can accept responsibility for any injury
or loss sustained as a result of
the use of this material.

Acknowledgements

All photographs by Sylvio Dokov.
Thanks to Dave Oliver, Ron Sergiew
and Gianni Peros for taking part in
the demonstrations.
Thanks to David Mitchell for helping
with the text.

A & C Black uses paper produced with
elemental chlorine-free pulp, harvested
from managed sustainable forests.

Typeset by ABM Typographics Ltd, Hull
Printed and bound in Great Britain by
The Bath Press, Bath

Contents

Introduction

What is tae kwon-do?

Tae kwon-do is a Korean phrase made from three parts. *Tae* means 'foot' (as in to destroy with), *kwon* means 'fist' and *Do* means 'way' (in the sense of 'path you should follow'). So *tae kwon-do* means 'Way of the foot and fist'. Tae kwon-do refers to a Korean fighting system which uses the hands and feet to deliver high energy impact techniques to the opponent. These techniques take the form of punches, strikes, kicks and blocks.

Tae kwon-do is rightly called a 'martial art' because it actually has been employed by the Korean military. Even in these days of long range weaponry, there are times when the soldier engages the enemy in hand-to-hand combat and it is under these circumstances that tae kwon-do has proved itself effective.

Tae kwon-do is also an exciting combat sport in which skills are tested in a rigorously controlled competition. Contestants wear safety padding on fists and feet, and impacts are 'pulled' to avoid injury. One form of tae kwon-do has now been accepted into the Olympic Games.

Tae kwon-do is a healthy, fitness-promoting activity for persons of all ages, encouraging through its regular practice both self-respect and self-discipline.

Where did tae kwon-do originate?

Tae kwon-do was developed in the Korean peninsula and several different sources contributed towards the art as it is practised today. Earliest of these sources is the Korean martial tradition itself. This developed in response to the many wars and battles which feature in Korea's long history. Another early source is probably Chinese, that country being Korea's nearest neighbour. From earliest times the Chinese developed and refined forms of combat by Buddhist monks and military attachés. The most recent source is Japanese, for the military of that country invaded Korea in 1907 and remained in occupation until 1945. The Japanese taught their fighting systems to Koreans in an effort to raise the latters' martial spirit.

Though tae kwon-do owes something to all these sources, what we now practise is a new system that reflects a truly unique blend of characteristics. Tae kwon-do kicking techniques are widely regarded as the most sophisticated in the martial world, and followers of other disciplines come to tae kwon-do to study them. Impact testing techniques also reach a peak in tae kwon-do.

The Tae Kwon-do Association of Great Britain

Tae kwon-do was introduced into the United Kingdom during 1967, but owing to subsequent political differences arising in Korea, first two then several competing groups came into existence. A number of these were and are dominated by foreign nationals with financial and political interests in what they are doing. A group of the most senior British tae kwon-do instructors eventually became so disillusioned with the situation that in 1983 they joined forces to form the Tae Kwon-do Association of Great Britain. The TAGB contains some of the world's top tae kwon-do performers, with several world, European and British champions.

Since its inauguration, the TAGB has grown to become the largest and most successful tae kwon-do practising organisation in Britain, with more than 12,000 members training in over 300 schools nationwide.

The TAGB is not just concerned with its own development. That is why it has played a leading role in the reunification of British tae kwon-do into one body. In 1988, the TAGB helped found the British Tae Kwon-do Council, this being the only governing body of tae kwon-do to be recognised by the Sports Council.

The TAGB also helped found Tae Kwon-do International, the object of which is to bring together tae kwon-do practitioners throughout the world. Tae Kwon-do International is non-political and it doesn't attempt to dictate to member countries how they must run their affairs. Since its foundation in 1993, Tae Kwon-do International has grown to become one of the biggest world tae kwon-do bodies. Its world championships are amongst the largest and best organised and it draws its participation from every continent.

The TAGB headquarters are: Redfield Leisure Centre, 163A Church Road, Redfield, Bristol BS5 9LA (tel: 0117 9551046).

The martial mind

Practice of tae kwon-do involves techniques which by their nature are potentially hazardous to your partners and to yourself. For this reason, training must involve both physical and mental discipline. Through self-discipline and respect you will develop both a sensitivity for the needs of others, and a modest pride in your own achievements.

Tae kwon-do is more than a mere fighting system. Its practice is intended to have a beneficial effect on your character; therefore your attitude is one of the most important factors in whether training will be successful or not. A TAGB student with the correct attitude will be polite in his dealings with other students and with the instructor.

Learn and put into practice the following points.

● Never tire of learning. Always be eager to learn and ask questions. A good student can learn anywhere and at any time. This is the secret of knowledge.

● Be prepared to make sacrifices both for your art and for your instructor. Many students wrongly believe that tae kwon-do training is a commodity which can be bought and sold with the payment of training fees. Such students are unwilling to take part in demonstrations, teaching, or work in the dojang. An instructor can afford to lose this type of student.

● Always set a good example to lower ranking students because they will regard you as a role model and copy your attitude, appearance, behaviour, etc.

● Always remember that your conduct outside the training hall (*dojang*), as well as inside it, reflects on the public image of tae kwon-do.

● Always be loyal and never criticise your instructor, tae kwon-do, or the teaching methods.

● Never be disrespectful to the instructor. Though you may disagree with him, first follow the instruction you have been given and raise the matter later.

● Practise the techniques you are taught and try to apply them.

● If you adopt a technique from another dojang and your instructor disapproves of it, then either discard the technique immediately, or transfer your club membership to the dojang it was learnt in.

● Ensure you have a good training record and always arrive before the scheduled start time for training.

Grading

For the newcomer to tae kwon-do, there is a long and arduous path to the Black Belt. This is defined by a training syllabus which introduces new techniques at regular intervals, so you are constantly being encouraged to improve your skills. At the end of a set period of practice time, you are assessed by means of a grading examination to see whether your standards have reached a specified level. If they have, then you are rewarded with a coloured belt. The following belt system is used by the TAGB.

● 10th & 9th kup.............White Belt.
● 8th & 7th kup.............Yellow Belt.
● 6th & 5th kup.............Green Belt.
● 4th & 3rd kup.............Blue Belt.
● 2nd & 1st kup.............Red Belt.
● The Black Belt, which is made up of *Dan* grades.

Never ask about taking the next grade, or expect to receive it. Preoccupation with advancement is a manifestation of the self-important ego, and that is something the practice of tae kwon-do attempts to suppress; it is only when the ego is diminished that you can truly behave without self-interest.

There will be times when you feel you cannot master a technique. This is inevitable given the high demands made by tae kwon-do on the abilities of each and every performer. The student who will eventually succeed is the one who keeps on trying; the one with enough motivation to push himself through all hardship and obstacles.

Courage is another essential ingredient for the tae kwon-do student. There are those who are afraid of the prospect of destruction testing or free sparring. This is natural and moderates otherwise reckless aggression, but too much fear can inhibit performance. You must first learn to defeat yourself before you ever expect to defeat others!

This brings us finally to the tenets of tae kwon-do.

● **Courtesy**   Always be polite to instructors, seniors and fellow students.
● **Integrity**   Always be honest with yourself, and know what is right and what is wrong.
● **Perseverance**   Never stop trying to achieve a goal.
● **Self-control**   Never lose your temper when you perform techniques against an opponent because this can be dangerous. Live, work and train within your capabilities.
● **Indomitable spirit**   Show courage and stick to your guns even in the face of overwhelming odds.

Etiquette

As you will have realised, tae kwon-do practice is closely associated with courtesy and respect. Begin with self-respect by ensuring that your training uniform (*dobok*) is clean, tidy and in good condition. The dobok is an important part of training because it brings everyone, regardless of wealth and social class, to the same level. Therefore always ensure you wear a uniform approved by the TAGB – see your instructor for details.

Wear the correct colour of belt and tie it neatly and correctly according to the following:

Fig. 1 Locate one end of the belt and take it across your stomach. The length of belt you take will be determined by experience.

Fig. 2 Wind the longer portion of the belt around your back and twice around you, and bring the other free end across your front.

Fig. 3 Tuck the left free end under both coils and bring it up . . .

Fig. 4 . . . then take it down over the front of the right free end.

Fig. 5 Tuck it under the right free end and through the loop. Then pull on both ends to draw the knot tight. If you have tied your belt correctly, then it will emerge from the knot in a quarter-to-three position. Both protruding lengths must be the same length. If they aren't, then untie the knot, go back to **fig. 1** and adjust the starting length.

You are now properly dressed to enter the dojang. Pause as you do and take up a formal attention stance (*charyot sogi*).

Fig. 6 Stand erect, hold your head up and bring your heels together. Place the palms of your hands flat on your thighs.

Fig. 7 *Below* Incline your head and shoulders forward as you perform a standing bow to the national flags. Make the bow smooth and pause a fraction at the lowest point before returning to an upright position. Note that you never at any time look down at the floor because though the bow is respectful, it is not obsequious.

If the instructor is already present, turn towards him and perform a second standing bow. You are then free to exchange greetings with the other students. When the lesson is due to start, the instructor will call students into lines. When they have all found their places and settled down, the class will perform a further standing bow to the instructor, and at the same time he will bow to them.

Always behave in a quiet and attentive way. Never talk or laugh loudly in the dojang. Apart from the need to exchange a few words of advice with your training partner or to speak to the instructor, it shouldn't be necessary for you to say anything. Don't lounge around or lean against walls, and when you sit down always cross your legs so they are out of the way.

At the conclusion of training, you must sit cross legged and meditate for one minute. Then the instructor will call the class to order and you will exchange standing bows. Pause at the exit to the dojang and perform a further bow before leaving.

You may be required to know The International Tae Kwon-do Oath, as follows:

> As a student of tae kwon-do
> I shall observe the tenets of tae kwon-do;
> I shall respect the instructor and seniors;
> I shall never misuse tae kwon-do;
> I shall be a champion of freedom and justice;
> I shall build a more peaceful world.

Getting ready to train

To receive all the benefits from tae kwon-do training, it is necessary to be fit enough to practise. If you find yourself preoccupied with just lasting through the session, then you will miss a good many of the techniques, and improve more slowly than fitter colleagues. Ideally you should be fit enough to cope with the pace of training, so your mind is free to concentrate on getting techniques right.

Being fit simply means being physically and mentally able to practise tae kwon-do. You may not be fit enough to lift 100 kilos but, since that doesn't form part of tae kwon-do training anyway, you won't miss it. You may not be fit enough to run a marathon in record time, or beat a sprinter over the 100-metre dash, yet still be ideally fit to practise tae kwon-do. This is because each activity requires a very specific mix of fitness factors. Much of the fitness you need for tae kwon-do will come from the training itself, though you will help things along by using specialist exercises.

The following series of exercises is commonly used throughout the TAGB, though the order in which they are performed may be considerably varied. Generally, instructors will begin with less arduous exercises and gradually increase intensity as your body becomes used to the workload.

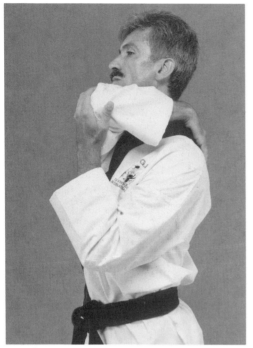

Fig. 8 Begin with a gentle shoulder stretch. Take your arm over the top of your shoulder and press it back firmly. Repeat this a number of times, then change arms.

Fig. 9 *Above, right.* Now raise both arms above your head and take one elbow with the other hand. Draw your elbow across. Repeat this a number of times, then change elbows.

Fig. 10 Take both arms forward in front of you. Circle the wrists, first one way, then the other.

Fig. 11 Drop into a squat with your hands resting on top of your knees.

Fig. 12 Straighten your legs and push back against the knees. Repeat this exercise several times.

Fig. 13 Press against your knees and rotate your ankle joints so the knees move in a circle. Circle first one way, then the other.

Fig. 14 Drop forward and press your palms to the floor. Fully straighten your knees to stretch the hamstrings.

13

Fig. 15 Lie on your back and steady yourself with your hands. Extend both legs fully and lift one 90° to the floor. Then drop it back, and at the same time lift the other.

Fig. 16 Remain on your back and let your legs separate under gravity. If the stretch becomes too painful, then lift your legs before relaxing them again. Be careful – this exercise can be a killer!

Fig. 17 Extend your left leg and put the sole of your right foot against the thigh. Take hold of your left ankle in both hands and draw your upper body down. Hold the stretch before returning to an upright position.

Fig. 18 Spread your legs as widely as possible, keeping the backs of your knees pressed firmly to the floor. Lean your upper body forward and try to touch the floor with your chest.

Fig. 19 Sit up and draw both heels into your groin. Take your feet in your hands and pull your head down. Hold the stretch at the lowest point and then release.

Fig. 20 Extend your left leg in front of you and your right behind you. Take your weight on the palms of your hands and lower yourself down into splits. Hold lowest position, then change lead legs and repeat.

Fig. 21 Turn your hips forward and drop into a box splits. This requires a high level of flexibility at the hips.

This concludes the first part of the opening exercise programme. Now you are ready to go on to something more vigorous.

Fig. 22 Lie on your back and bend your knees. Put your hands behind your head and curl forward in a sit-up. Repeat this action several times.

Fig. 23 Vary the previous exercise by twisting your trunk as you sit up, so each elbow touches the opposite knee.

Fig. 24 Vary the exercise again, this time by bringing both knees up to meet your elbows.

Fig. 25 Close your hands into fists and assume a press-up position with your back absolutely straight. Using the fists helps condition them for later use.

Fig. 26 Bend your elbows and lower your body until your chest brushes the floor. Then thrust yourself back to starting position again. Repeat this action several times.

Fig. 27 Drop from a standing position into a crouch. Place your palms on the floor.

Fig. 28 Shoot your legs out behind you and then jump straight back into a crouch again.

Fig. 29 Jump up, so both feet leave the floor, then drop down into a crouch and repeat the whole cycle. This exercise is known as 'burpees' and it is quite strenuous.

19

By now you should be thoroughly warmed up and ready to begin training. Later during the session, the instructor may introduce a second session of exercises, this time with the object of increasing some aspect of fitness such as flexibility. Partner stretches are often used for this purpose.

Partner stretches require co-operation. Your partner will help you reach the limits of your flexibility and hold you there for the necessary physiological changes to take place. He must not take you past your limits, since this may cause injury. This means releasing pressure the instant you tell him to. Pressure must be applied firmly and smoothly, and all jerkiness must be avoided since this also can cause actual injury.

Fig. 30 Sit down and spread your legs wide. Press the back of your legs against the floor and don't bend your knees! Your partner stands close behind and puts his hands on the small of your back. He exerts a steady pressure to hold you in the lowest point of the stretch.

Fig. 31 Draw your heels in close to your groin and take hold of your feet. Your partner leans foward, places his hands against the inside of your knees, and presses firmly down.

Fig. 32 Sit facing your partner and put the soles of your feet together with his. Bend your knees at first, so you can take hold of each other's wrists. Then straighten your legs fully and take it in turns to draw the other forward.

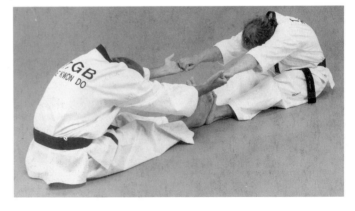

Fig. 33 Allow your legs to open fully and take hold of your partner's belt. He then leans back until his head touches the floor.

Fig. 34 Lie on your back and extend your leg upwards. Your partner takes the ankle and pushes it forward in a hamstring stretch. Hold the point of maximum stretch, then repeat. Change legs and continue the exercise.

Fig. 35 Stand sideways-on to your partner and straighten your leg, resting the heel on his shoulder. He then slowly stands upright. Hold the stretch, then change legs.

Fig. 36 Turn your hips until they face the opponent and rest your Achilles tendon on his shoulder. Straighten your knee and take your ankle in both hands as your partner steadies you. Then draw your head forward and down to the knee. Repeat several times and change legs.

Just as you warmed up before training started, so it is a good idea to warm down before returning to your everyday life. Repeat the initial exercises at a gradually slowing tempo and the continued stretching will help move lactic acid from fatigued muscles. This in turn will minimise stiffness and muscle soreness the day after training.

The final part of the warm down is the period of seated meditation before the instructor calls the class to final order. Use this time to relax all your muscles and empty your mind, so you don't leave the dojang on an adrenalin high.

White Belt (10th kup)

White signifies innocence like that of the novice student who has no previous knowledge of tae kwon-do.

The techniques contained in this syllabus are the same for all clubs within the TAGB, though the order in which they are taught may vary considerably.

The first thing you must learn is how to form a correct forefist (*ap joomuk*). Look at your fist and you will see it has a rounded shape, meaning that you can't land on all your knuckles with equal force. Tae kwon-do uses the two largest knuckles to concentrate force over a small area, making the punch particularly effective (**fig. 37**).

Making a fist

To make a correct fist, first extend your fingers and thumb, then fold the fingers down until the tips contact the pad of flesh running along the top of your palm. Close the fist and lock the fingers in place with your thumb.

Fig. 37 The correct forefist.

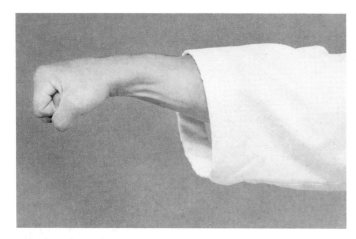

Fig. 38 A correct fist shows a 90° angle between the folded fingers and the back of the hand. The thumb locks the fist closed and the forearm and fist are in one line.

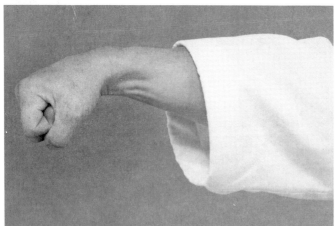

Fig. 39 Here the fist has dropped so it is no longer in line with the forearm. This will cause painful flexions of the wrist during heavy impacts.

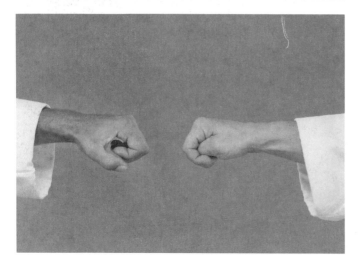

Fig. 40 The fist on the left is not fully closed, so painful impact will be made with the middle joints of the fingers, instead of the knuckles. Help form a correct fist shape by performing press-ups on the closed fists (see earlier). A very serious (and painful!) mistake is to enclose the thumb within the fist. This can lead to a dislocation.

Basic punching exercises

Tae kwon-do punches use a corkscrew action that turns the fist from palm-upwards facing to palm-downwards facing as impact is about to be made. Practise this twisting action by means of single arm punching from parallel ready stance (*narani sogi*).

Fig. 41 Begin from attention stance by stepping out to the side with the left foot until the outer edges of both feet are a shoulder width apart and parallel to each other. Close your hands into fists and extend your arms slightly forward.

25

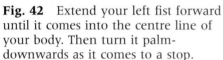

Fig. 42 Extend your left fist forward until it comes into the centre line of your body. Then turn it palm-downwards as it comes to a stop.

Fig. 43 *Above, right.* Keep the fist turned palm-downwards as you draw it smoothly back.

Fig. 44 *Right.* Rotate the fist palm-upwards as it comes to a stop against the side of the body. Then push the fist forward and repeat the cycle. Continue practice with your right hand.

The object is to punch smoothly and without undue shoulder movement into the centre line of your body. The fist-twisting action comes at either end of the move.

Punching with both fists

Having mastered that simple exercise, you will next move to punching in a co-ordinated manner with both fists. In this case, one fist is extending at the same time and speed as the other is drawing back. Imagine you are holding one end of your belt in either hand and it is looped around a pole. As you pull back one fist, so the other will be drawn forward an equal distance at an equal speed. This co-ordination is what you must aim for. Both fists twist simultaneously at the end of each punch, one turning palm-upwards, the other palm-downwards.

Fig. 45 Begin the exercise by stepping to the side with the left foot and taking up sitting stance (*annun sogi*) from parallel stance. Sitting stance is one-and-a-half shoulder widths apart, and the feet are turned in slightly. Push your knees outwards so they come to overlie the ankles. Pull both fists back to the ribs.

27

Fig. 46 Extend your left fist into the mid-line of your body at shoulder height, and turn it palm-downwards.

Fig. 47 *Above, right.* Draw your left fist back sharply and at exactly the same time and speed, extend the right fist so they pass each other at the mid-way point.

Fig. 48 Continue drawing your left fist back and turn it palm-upwards as it comes to a stop. At exactly the same time, the right fist twists palm-downwards and also comes to a stop. Breathe out sharply in the form of a shout (*kihap*).

Kihap

Kihap is used in conjunction with many forceful techniques. It is not made by the muscles of the chest; rather it comes from the diaphragm, being the same kind of staccato noise made when, say, pushing a car. Its name derives from the union of the body giving maximum effort with the mind that is intensely focused on the task in hand.

Walking stance

Next you will need to learn walking stance (*gunnun sogi*).

Fig. 49 Begin from parallel ready stance by stepping forward a distance equivalent to one-and-a-half shoulder widths. This fully extends the knee of the trailing leg. The stance is also a shoulder width wide. Bend your leading knee until it comes to overlie the heel. Weight is distributed evenly between both feet.

Fig. 50 The instructor on the left ha⸱ not fully extended his trailing leg and the knee is bent. This is incorrect. On the right, the stance has no width, making it unstable laterally.

Obverse punch

Obverse punch (*baro jirugi*) is a powerful technique delivered as part of a lunging movement (**fig. 51**). Note that the punching arm and leading leg are on the same side of the body, and walking stance is used to give the technique great penetration and stability.

Fig. 51 Obverse punch (*baro jirugi*).

Fig. 52 Begin from ready stance by sliding the right foot forward. At the same time, withdraw your right fist and turn it palm-upwards.

Fig. 53   As you settle into right walking stance, so you strongly pull back your left fist and punch with the right. Don't punch too early or you'll be pulled off balance, and don't punch too late or you will lose the energy bonus provided by your moving body.

Fig. 54   *Above, right.* Hold your right fist out as you slide the left foot forward in shallow arc. Make sure you keep your knees bent or you will bob up and down. A slight up-and-down movement is correct, though this should not be over-emphasised.

Fig. 55   Begin to draw back your right fist as the left moves forward . . .

CONTINUED

Fig. 56 . . . and complete the punch. Additional power is generated by the body dropping slightly into the final stance position.

Fig. 57 Leaning forward or leading with your punching shoulder are two of the most common faults of obverse punch.

Eventually you will run out of space. At that point, you can either repeat the punch as you step backwards, or you can perform a turn-and-punch combination. Holding your punch out, slide your front foot across, look over your shoulder and then slide the back foot across. Then swivel your hips and punch as the turn comes to a stop.

Reverse punch

Reverse punch (*bandae jirugi*) is similar to obverse punch except that the punching arm is opposite to the lead foot; so if you step forward with your *left* foot, then you punch with the *right* fist.

Fig. 58   Begin from parallel ready stance by sliding your left foot forward into walking stance.

Fig. 59   *Above, right.* The new stance is close to completion as the left fist draws back and the right thrusts out. The fists have already begun to twist into their final positions.

Fig. 60   The right fist is now fully extended and the stance is solid.

Inner forearm middle block

Next we move on to study the first pair of a series of blocks. These deflect the opponent's attack and prevent it from reaching its target. The first to be practised is inner forearm middle block (*an palmok makgi*). This uses the thumb-side of the forearm to sweep an incoming technique to the side (**fig. 61**). Like the punching techniques described before, this block makes use of the simultaneous pull-back on the non-blocking arm.

Fig. 61 Inner forearm middle block (*an palmok makgi*).

Fig. 62 Begin from ready stance by stepping forward into left walking stance. Bring your left arm back and across the upper part of your chest. Extend the right fist forward over the left elbow.

34

Fig. 63 Begin to draw back the right fist, using this action to power the block. Your left forearm begins to swing in an upwards-moving arc.

Fig. 64 *Below.* Your right fist has been pulled back and has come to a stop. Your left forearm has swung upwards like the windscreen wiper of a car. The blocking fist twists knuckles-forward, and it is held at shoulder height with the elbow bent to 90°. This angle gives the widest and deepest possible sweeping action.

Fig. 65

One of the most common mistakes with this block is to bring the blocking arm to the inside of and above the arm that is to be pulled back (**fig. 65**). You must always hold the blocking arm to the outside of the withdrawing arm.

Moving forward inner forearm middle block

Once you can perform the blocking action in stationary mode, the next step is to practise it as you move forward.

Fig. 66 *Left.* Begin from parallel ready stance by sliding your left foot forward and bringing your left arm across your upper chest as before.

Fig. 67 *Right.* As the stance completes, so the right fist draws back to your side and the left swings up and across.

Fig. 68 Then step forward with your right foot and bring your right arm across your upper chest.

Fig. 69 Swing the right forearm up and complete the block.

Turning inner forearm middle block

Eventually you will run out of space and have to turn around.

Fig. 70 Slide your leading foot inwards.

Fig. 71 *Below, left.* Look over your shoulder and slide your trailing foot across. Your left arm is cocked ready to perform the block, the right overlies it. Note the angles at which the two fists are held.

Fig. 72 *Below.* Twist your hips, draw back your right fist and perform the block.

Lower outer forearm block

Next block to practise is lower outer forearm block (*bakat palmok makgi*).
Whereas the previous block used the thumb-side of the forearm to deflect an
attack, this block uses the little finger side (**fig. 73**) in a down-swinging arc.

Fig. 73

Fig. 74 Begin from walking stance by bringing your left arm up and across your upper chest so it overlies the right biceps. The right fist is brought forward and to the *outside* of the blocking arm. Begin drawing back your right arm as the left starts to move downwards and out.

Fig. 75 *Above, right.* Here the right fist is nearly back to the hip and the block almost completed.

Fig. 76 The block is completed when the leading arm comes to lie just above the knee.

Moving forward lower outer forearm block

Once you have understood the action, the next step is to practise the block while moving forward.

Fig. 77 Begin from ready stance by sliding forward on the left foot. Turn your hips away and raise your arms so the left crosses your upper chest and the right overlies it.

Fig. 78 As the back leg fully straightens, so the withdrawing fist comes to a stop and the block is completed.

Turning lower outer forearm block

Eventually you will run out of space, so perform a turn coupled with the block.

Fig. 79 Slide across with the leading foot.

Fig. 80 Look over your shoulder, slide your trailing foot across and raise your arms in preparation for the block. CONTINUED

41

Fig. 81   Turn your hips strongly and perform the block.

Fig. 82

Make sure you do not block directly down on to a fast rising shin (**fig. 82**). Instead, strike into the *side* of the shin. Also, bring the blocking fist down close to the lead knee, or you will leave a gap for an incoming kick. Block right across your body, or you will simply deflect the kick into your side. Avoid over-blocking too, since this is inefficient.

Inner forearm block and reverse punch

This is a simple linear combination of a block and a punch. Blocks are defensive techniques and it is usual to follow them with a counter attack.

Fig. 83 Step forward into right walking stance and perform inner forearm block.

Fig. 84 Pull back your leading hand and thrust your left fist out in a mid-section reverse punch. CONTINUED

Fig. 85 Step through with the trailing leg and bring your arms up in preparation for the next inner forearm block.

Fig. 86 *Above, right.* Perform the block and follow it with . . .

Fig. 87 Reverse punch to mid-section.

Eventually you will run out of space so either perform the combination as you step back, or execute an about turn.

Turning inner forearm block and reverse punch

Fig. 88   Slide your leading foot across.

Fig. 89   Look over your shoulder and bring your arms into pre-blocking position as you slide your trailing foot across.

Fig. 90   Perform the block, then . . .

Fig. 91   . . . add the punch to complete the combination.

45

Four-directional punching

Four-directional punching (*sajo jirugi*) takes punching and blocking combinations a step further by combining them with both stepping and turning movements to create a whole series of moves. Practising it will help with co-ordination, direction changing and breathing control.

Fig. 92 Begin from parallel ready stance by sliding forward on your right foot and performing right obverse punch.

Fig. 93 Draw back your right foot and raise both arms in preparation for a low-section outer forearm block.

Fig. 94 Turn 90° left, then slide out with your left foot and block with your left forearm.

Fig. 95 *Above, right.* Step forward with your right foot and perform right obverse punch.

Fig. 96 Draw back your right foot, turn and prepare to block with your left arm. CONTINUED

47

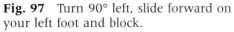

Fig. 97 Turn 90° left, slide forward on your left foot and block.

Fig. 98 *Above, right.* Step forward into right walking stance and perform right obverse punch.

Fig. 99 Continue turning to the left and perform a low-section outer forearm block.

Fig. 100 Step forward into right walking stance and perform right obverse punch with *kihap* to complete the exercise. Then draw up your left foot and assume parallel ready stance once more.

The exercise should be repeated on the other side by stepping forward with the *left* leg and punching with the left fist. Then turn to the right, slide your right foot forward and perform a low-section outer forearm block. Continue turning to the right, blocking with the right fist and punching with the left until you have completed the exercise.

Sajo jirugi (2) is identical to the previous exercise except that middle-section inner forearm block is used instead of lower-section outer forearm block.

Fig. 101   Begin from parallel stance by sliding forward on your right foot and performing right obverse punch.

Fig. 102   *Above, right.* Draw back your right foot and raise both arms in preparation for a middle-section inner forearm block.

Fig. 103   Turn 90°, slide your left foot out, draw back your right fist and block with your left forearm.

Fig. 104 Step forward with your right foot and perform right obverse punch.

Fig. 105 *Below, left.* Draw back your right foot, turn 90°, and block with your left forearm.

Fig. 106 *Below.* Step forward into right walking stance and perform right obverse punch. CONTINUED

Fig. 107 Continue turning to the left and perform a middle-section inner forearm block.

Fig. 108 Step forward into right walking stance and perform right obverse punch with *kihap* to complete the exercise. Then draw up your left foot and assume parallel ready stance once more.

Sajo jirugi (2) must also be practised on the other side by stepping forward with the *left* leg and punching with the left fist. Then turn to the right, slide your right foot forward and perform a middle-section inner forearm block. Continue turning to the right, blocking with the right fist and punching with the left until you have completed the exercise.

Front rising kick exercise

Four-directional punching concludes the hand techniques part of this grading requirement, and we move on finally to leg techniques.

Ap cha olligi is a hip mobility exercise that is practised as part of the formal syllabus.

Fig. 109 Begin from left walking stance, taking your arms out to the side and closing them into fists.

Fig. 110 Keep your knee straight as you swing your right leg forward and up. Aim to butt the knee against the front of your right shoulder. Note the way the foot is held, with all the toes drawn back. CONTINUED

Fig. 111 This illustrates two of the most common mistakes: bending the knee on the kicking leg, and lifting the arms/shoulders.

Side rising kick exercise

Yop cha olligi is a second hip mobility exercise practised as part of the formal syllabus.

Fig. 112 Take up sitting stance and turn your head to the right. Hold your arms out to the side and close them into fists. Step behind your right foot into x-stance (*kyocha sogi*). Keep both knees well bent, so you don't bob up and down. CONTINUED

Fig. 113 Swing your right foot in an ascending arc, allowing your upper body to lean the opposite way as you do. Your heel reaches the highest point and the little toe-edge of your foot leads. This foot position will be covered in greater detail when we come to practise side kick.

White Belt (9th kup)

Sitting stance and double punch

Begin from parallel ready stance by stepping to either side into sitting stance. Pull both fists back to your sides, then extend the left arm fully and rotate the fist palm-downwards. Each time the instructor calls, perform first a right then a left punch. The punches follow each other quickly, the pull-back of one helping power the delivery of the other. After you have performed this combination a number of times, change your starting fist and repeat the exercise.

L-stance

L-stance (*niunja sogi*) figures heavily in this part of the syllabus. Begin from parallel ready stance by stepping forward a distance equivalent to one-and-a-half shoulder widths with your left leg. Note that there is almost no width component to this stance and the heels are nearly in line. The lead foot points very slightly inwards and the rear foot is turned 90° outwards. Move your body weight until 70% is carried by the rear foot and 30% by the leading foot. Bend your rear knee until it overlies the toes and adjust the leading knee accordingly (**fig. 114**).

Fig. 114 CONTINUED

Fig. 115 Here the rear foot has been turned outwards too far. This is a common error in L-stance.

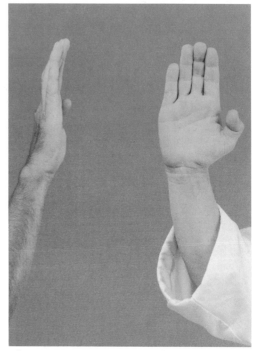

Fig. 116

Knife hand

Knife hand (*sonkal*) uses the little finger-edge of the palm to concentrate impact force over a narrow strip. Knife hand may be used both to block a technique and to strike the opponent with.

The hand is opened and the fingers slightly cupped. Bend the middle and ring finger slightly inwards and bring the thumb close to but not touching the base of the index finger (**fig. 116**).

Fig. 117 *Right.* This shows incorrect hand shapes for knife hand. The one on the left is bent at the wrist; that on the right has the fingers separated.

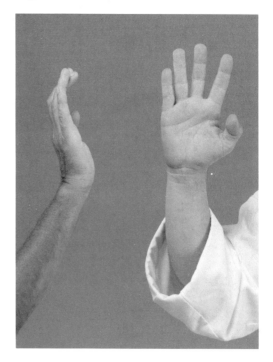

Knife hand strike

Knife hand strike (*sonkal taerigi*) uses a pull-back action similar to that used with some of the blocks.

Fig. 118 Begin from ready stance by stepping forward into right L-stance. Bring your left arm back and across the upper part of your chest. Extend the fingers and rotate the hand until the palm is turned towards your face. The right fist is brought forward and to the outside of the left forearm. It is turned palm-downwards.

Fig. 119 Draw back the right fist, using this action to power the strike. Your left forearm swings outwards in a horizontal arc and the hand turns palm-down-wards.

Guarding block

Guarding block (*daebi makgi*) swings both arms together across the body, taking an incoming technique on the little finger-side of the forearm.

Fig. 120 Begin from left L-stance with your right arm leading. Bend your elbow so the fist is the same height as your shoulder. Bring the left fist across your chest and turn it palm-upwards.

Fig. 121 *Above, right.* Step forward with your left foot and take both arms well to the right. The left palm of the closed fist is turned towards your face. The little finger-side of the right fist is further from you.

Fig. 122 Swing both arms together across your body and rotate your left fist until the knuckles are uppermost, and your right fist until the knuckles turn down.

Turning guarding block

Eventually you will run out of space. When this happens, either perform the block as you step back, or turn about-face.

Fig. 123 Slide your front foot inwards while maintaining your guard.

Fig. 124 Your left foot hardly moves at all, except to rotate, and your arms swing in unison across your chest.

Inner forearm middle block from L-stance

We covered *an palmok makgi* in the previous grade. Just to recap, this uses the thumb-side of the forearm to sweep an incoming technique to the side. The non-punching arm withdraws strongly to help power the blocking action.

Fig. 125 Begin from parallel ready stance by stepping forward into right L-stance. Bring your left arm back and across the upper part of your chest. Extend the right fist forward over the left elbow.

Fig. 126 Draw back the right fist, using this action to power the block. Your left forearm swings in an upwards-moving arc like the windscreen wiper of a car. The blocking fist twists knuckles-forward and it is held at shoulder height with the elbow bent to 90°.

62

Outer block to mid-section

Outer block (*bakat palmok makgi*) uses the little finger-side of the forearm to accomplish deflection. The completed block looks similar to the guarding block we practised earlier, though outer block uses a pulling-back action of the non-blocking fist rather than moving both arms together in the same direction.

Fig. 127 Begin from parallel ready stance by stepping forward into left L-stance. Bring your right arm back and across the upper part of your chest, turning the palm towards your face. The left fist is brought forward and to the outside of the right forearm. The left fist is turned so the knuckles are towards your face.

Fig. 128 Draw back the left fist, using this action to power the block. Your right forearm swings across your body in a horizontal arc, and the wrist twists until the knuckles turn upwards.

Inwards moving forearm block

Anuro makgi also uses the little finger-side of the forearm to block, though it is rather more powerful than the previous example.

Fig. 129 Begin from right L-stance, pulling your right fist back and extending the left forward. Rotate the left forearm until the palm faces upwards and then bend the elbow to approximately 90°. The fist is now the same height as your shoulder.

Fig. 130 *Above, right.* Begin to step into left L-stance and as you do, rotate your left fist palm-downwards and begin to withdraw it. Your right fist rises and turns palm-outwards.

Fig. 131 Complete your step into left L-stance and fully withdraw the left fist. Your right forearm sweeps horizontally across your body and turns palm towards you as the block concludes.

Back fist strike

As its name suggests, back fist (*dung joomuk*) uses the back of the two major knuckles in a swinging strike to the target. We are considering it at this point rather than earlier on because it is linked here with the block we have just practised.

Fig. 132 Complete inwards moving outer forearm block as described in the previous sequence. The opponent's obverse punch is deflected outwards. CONTINUED

65

Fig. 133 Bring the blocking arm back and over your left shoulder, turning it palm-downwards. The left arm is brought forward and to the outside of the right arm. That too is turned palm-downwards.

Fig. 134 Draw your left fist back to the hip, using this action to power a circular strike with the right back fist into the bridge of the opponent's nose.

Low block and rising block

Rising block (*chookyo makgi*) sweeps the face and forehead clear of attacks (**fig. 135**). It achieves this by lifting into the path of the incoming technique. The blocking forearm then rotates until the little finger-side is uppermost. In this part of the syllabus, rising block is combined with the by now familiar low-section outer forearm block.

Fig. 135   Rising block.   CONTINUED

67

Fig. 136 Step forward into left walking stance and bring your left arm to the side of your head. The right extends forward on the outside of the left, being also rotated until the thumb points downwards.

Fig. 137 *Above, right.* The right fist withdraws sharply to the hip, this action helping to power a low-section forearm block.

Fig. 138 Twist your hips sharply clockwise and bring your left fist palm-upwards in front of your chest. Your right fist is taken palm-downwards to the outside position.

Fig. 139 Turn your hips anti-clockwise, using this action to help thrust the left arm into a rising block.

Fig. 140 This shows some common mistakes of rising block. The person on the left has taken his elbow too far to the side, so the head is not fully protected. The one on the right has obscured his own vision. Keep the blocking elbow close to the side of your head but lift the forearm so it clears your vision.

Front kick

Front kick (*ap chagi*) strikes with the ball of the foot (*ap kumchi*). Note how the ankle joint is fully extended, so the instep is in line with the shin (**fig. 141**).

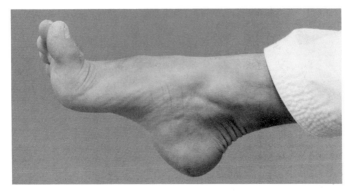

Fig. 141

Fig. 142 Begin from left walking stance with your left fist extended and the right brought back to the hip. The trailing right foot lifts rapidly and the knee rises to point at the target.

Fig. 143 The lower foot is then thrust out and the back arches as the hips thrust forward behind the kicking action.

Fig. 144 *Below, left.* Here the toes have not been pulled back. This is a dangerous mistake which can result in injury.

Fig. 145 *Below.* Failing to extend the ankle joint fully is another common mistake. Here the kick is striking with the sole of the foot.

Front kick and double punch

This gives practice at combining kicks with punches.

Fig. 146 Begin from left walking stance by extending the left arm downwards in a forearm block position.

Fig. 147 Bring the right knee up and forward, and perform a front kick.

Fig. 148 Drop the spent kick forward and settle into right walking stance, but even as you land thrust out your right fist in an obverse punch.

Fig. 149 Withdraw your right fist, using this action to help power a left reverse punch to mid-section.

Chon Ji

Chon Ji means literally 'Heaven and Earth'. In the Orient it is interpreted as the creation of the world, or the beginning of human history. Therefore, it is the initial pattern played by the beginner. This pattern consists of two similar parts, one to represent Heaven and the other the Earth. It has 19 moves.

Fig. 150 Begin from parallel ready stance by turning your head to the left, as you catch sight of the imaginary opponent.

Fig. 151 Step out to the left and turn into left walking stance while performing a downwards lower outer forearm block.

Fig. 152 Step forward and perform right obverse punch.

Fig. 153 *Below, left.* Twist your hips in a clockwise direction, taking the right foot diagonally back behind the left foot. Turn your hips strongly and perform a lower outer forearm block.

Fig. 154 *Below.* Step forward with the left foot and perform obverse punch. CONTINUED

Fig. 155   Move the left foot to the side and turn your hips through 90°. Perform downwards lower outer forearm block.

Fig. 156   *Above, right.* Step forward with the right foot and perform obverse punch.

Fig. 157   Step diagonally through with your right foot, so you turn 180°. Perform downwards outer forearm block.

Fig. 158 Step forward and perform left obverse punch.

Fig. 159 *Above, right.* Slide your left foot back and turn your hips into right L-stance. Perform left middle inner forearm block.

Fig. 160 Step forward with your right foot and perform obverse punch.

CONTINUED

Fig. 161   Bring your lead foot diagonally back and turn your hips strongly into left L-stance. Perform right middle inner forearm block.

Fig. 162   *Above, right.* Step forward with your left foot and perform obverse punch to mid-section.

Fig. 163   Move your lead foot to the left and turn your hips strongly into right L-stance. Perform left middle inner forearm block.

Fig. 164 Step forward with your right foot and perform obverse punch to mid-section.

Fig. 165 Bring your right foot diagonally back and around, turning strongly into left L-stance. Perform right middle inner forearm block.

Fig. 166 Step forward into left walking stance and perform obverse punch to mid-section.

CONTINUED

79

Fig. 167 Step forward again, performing a second obverse punch.

Fig. 168 Draw back your right foot and perform left obverse punch.

Fig. 169 Draw back your left foot and perform right obverse punch with *kihap*. Complete the pattern by sliding your left foot forward into ready stance.

Three-step sparring

Like patterns, three-step sparring (*sambo matsoki*) presents an opportunity to practise your techniques with safety. In this case, however, those techniques are tested against a partner. To minimise the possibility of injury, both the attack and response are known beforehand by both partners. The attacking partner performs the same technique three times and the defending partner makes the same set response each time. Following his response to the third attack, the defending partner then adds a counter attack to complete the sequence.

Repeating the same attack/response three times not only gives practice with techniques but it also helps you judge both distance and timing.

Three-step sparring (1)

Fig. 170 Face each other in attention stance, then perform a standing bow.

Fig. 171 Step into parallel ready stance and close your hands into fists. CONTINUED

81

Fig. 172 The partner who is to perform the first series of attacks measures the distance between you by stepping into right walking stance.

Fig. 173 The attacker withdraws his leading leg and returns to ready stance. He slides back his right foot and performs *kihap*. Respond with *kihap* to show you are ready.

Fig. 174   The attacker now steps forward and performs right obverse punch. Step back with your right foot and respond with middle inner forearm block.

Fig. 175   The attacker performs a second obverse punch, this time with the left fist. Respond as before by stepping back and using middle inner forearm block.   CONTINUED

Fig. 176 The attacker then makes the third and final obverse punch to which you respond by simply stepping back and using middle inner forearm block.

Fig. 177 Complete the sequence with a reverse punch to mid-section, and don't forget the *kihap*.

Step forward into parallel ready stance as your partner simultaneously withdraws. The sequence is then repeated except that this time you take the attacking role.

Three-step sparring (2)

As before, the partner who is to perform the first series of attacks measures the distance between you by stepping into right walking stance. Then he withdraws his leading leg and returns to ready stance. He slides back his right foot and performs *kihap*. Respond with *kihap* to show you are ready.

Fig. 178   The attacker steps forward and performs right obverse punch. Step back with your left foot into left L-stance and respond with middle inner forearm block.   CONTINUED

Fig. 179 The attacker performs a second obverse punch, this time with left fist. Respond as before by stepping back and using middle inner forearm block.

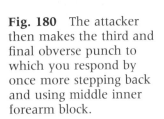

Fig. 180 The attacker then makes the third and final obverse punch to which you respond by once more stepping back and using middle inner forearm block.

Fig. 181 Complete the sequence by sliding your rear foot to the left. Bring your right hand near your left ear and take the left fist forward.

Fig. 182 Now slide your right foot to the left, pull back your left fist and perform knife hand strike to the side of your partner's neck. Don't forget the *kihap*!

As before, you should step forward into parallel ready stance while your partner simultaneously withdraws into ready stance. Change roles and repeat the sequence.

Three-step sparring (3)

Begin in the same way as the previous two sequences.

Fig. 183 The attacker steps forward and performs right obverse punch. Step back with your left foot into left L-stance and respond with middle inwards moving outer forearm block.

Fig. 184 *Above, right.* The attacker performs a second obverse punch, this time with the left fist. Respond as before by stepping back and using middle inwards moving forearm block.

Fig. 185 The attacker then makes the third and final obverse punch to which you respond by once more stepping back and using middle inwards moving forearm block.

Fig. 186 Bring your right fist near your left ear, and extend your left fist forward.

Fig. 187 *Below.* Use *kihap* as you draw back your left fist and perform back fist to the bridge of your partner's nose.

Conclude by stepping forward into parallel ready stance as your partner simultaneously withdraws into ready stance. Change roles and repeat the sequence.

Yellow Belt (8th kup)

Yellow signifies Earth, from which a plant sprouts and takes root as tae kwon-do foundation is being laid.

Knife hand guarding block

Sonkal daebi makgi is very similar to the guarding block we covered in the previous syllabus except it is performed with open hand.

Fig. 188 Begin from left L-stance with your right arm leading. Step forward with your left foot and take both arms well to the right. The palm of the open left hand is turned towards your face. The palm of the right hand is turned away from you.

Fig. 189 Swing both arms together across your body and rotate your left hand until the palm turns away from you. The right arm swings across your chest and turns palm-upwards to complete the block.

Fig. 190 Tilting the wrist back is a common fault of knife hand block . . .

Fig. 191 . . . as is dropping the hand too far forward.

Twin outer forearm block

Twin outer forearm block (*sang palmok makgi*) uses both arms to deflect two simultaneous punches (**fig. 192**).

Fig. 192

Fig. 193 Begin from right L-stance by drawing your leading left arm across your chest. Turn the palm of the closed fist towards you. The right arm overlies the left and that too has the palm turned towards you.

Fig. 195   Both forearms are parallel in a correctly performed block. In this case, the lead block has dropped and the elbow of the trailing block is too far away from the head it is supposed to be protecting.

Fig. 194   The left arm moves across the front and rotates palm-down-wards. At the same time, your right arm lifts and the fist rotates until the little finger-side is uppermost.

Fig. 196   Again, the forearms are not parallel. The lead block is bent too sharply back towards you and the right forearm has dropped until it obscures your vision.

93

Dan Gun

The pattern *Dan Gun* is named after the legendary founder of Korea who established the country in 2333 BC. Dan Gun contains 21 movements arranged to the following plan.

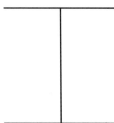

Fig. 197 Begin from parallel ready stance with a glance to the left.

Fig. 198 *Below, left.* Slide your left foot to the left and turn into L-stance. At the same time perform left guarding block with knife hand.

Fig. 199 Step forward into right walking stance and perform a high-section obverse punch.

94

Fig. 200 Step diagonally back with your right foot and turn into left L-stance. At the same time, perform right guarding block with knife hand.

Fig. 201 *Above, right.* Step forward into walking stance with your left foot and perform a high-section obverse punch.

Fig. 202 Step to the left with your lead foot and turn 90° while performing a lower-section outer forearm block.

CONTINUED

Fig. 203 Step forward into right walking stance and perform a high-section obverse punch.

Fig. 204 *Above, right.* Step forward into left walking stance and perform a high-section obverse punch.

Fig. 205 Step forward into right walking stance and perform a high-section obverse punch.

Fig. 206 Step diagonally through with the left leg and perform a twin forearm block from right L-stance.

Fig. 207 *Above, right.* Step forward into right walking stance and perform a high-section obverse punch.

Fig. 208 Step diagonally through with the right leg and perform a twin forearm block from left L-stance. CONTINUED

97

Fig. 209 Step forward into left walking stance and perform a high-section obverse punch.

Fig. 210 *Below, left.* Step to the left with the leading foot so you turn 90°, and perform a low-section outer forearm block.

Fig. 211 *Below.* With scarcely a pause, lift your left arm into a rising block.

Fig. 212 Step into right walking stance and perform a rising block with your right forearm.

Fig. 213 *Above, right.* Step into left walking stance and perform a further rising block.

Fig. 214 Step into right walking stance and perform a final rising block.

CONTINUED

Fig. 215 Turn into right L-stance and strike with left knife hand.

Fig. 216 Step forward into right walking stance and perform a high-section obverse punch.

Fig. 217 Bring the right foot back and around, turning into left L-stance and striking with knife hand.

Fig. 218 Step forward into left walking stance and perform a final high-section obverse punch to complete the pattern. Then draw back your left foot into parallel ready stance.

Three-step sparring (4)

Begin as before from parallel ready stance. Measure the distance between you and your opponent, then return to ready stance. The opponent steps into left walking stance and performs a low-section outer forearm block. Remain waiting in parallel ready stance.

Fig. 219 Your opponent steps forward into right walking stance and performs obverse punch. Step back quickly with your left leg and perform a mid-section inner forearm block.

Fig. 220 The opponent steps into left walking stance and performs a second obverse punch. Step back smartly into right L-stance and use mid-section inner forearm block. CONTINUED

101

Fig. 221 Your opponent steps forward into right walking stance and performs a final obverse punch. Step back with your left leg and perform a mid-section inner forearm block.

Fig. 222 *Below, left.* Step forward with your left leg into sitting stance and measure the opponent's distance with your left fist. Keep your blocking forearm in position.

Fig. 223 *Below.* Draw back your blocking hand and . . .

Fig. 224 . . . punch with first your right fist . . .

Fig. 225 . . . then your left in a fast 'one-two' sequence.

Three-step sparring (5)

Fig. 226 Your opponent steps forward into right walking stance and performs obverse punch. Step back quickly with your right leg and perform a mid-section outer forearm block.

Fig. 227 The opponent steps into left walking stance and performs a second obverse punch. Step back smartly into L-stance and use mid-section outer forearm block.

Fig. 228 Slide your right foot forward into sitting stance and take the opponent's obverse punch on your left outer forearm. At the same time punch to the side of the opponent's jaw (see **fig. 229** for close-up).

Fig. 229

Three-step sparring (6)

Fig. 230 Your opponent steps forward into right walking stance and performs obverse punch. Step back quickly with your right leg and perform a mid-section knife hand guarding block.

Fig. 231 The opponent steps into left walking stance and performs a second obverse punch. Step back smartly into left L-stance and use mid-section knife hand guarding block again.

Fig. 232 Slide your right foot forward into sitting stance and take the opponent's obverse punch on your left knife hand. At the same time strike to the side of the opponent's neck with knife hand.

Fig. 233 This is a close-up of the combination block and strike.

Yellow Belt (7th kup)

Vertical stance

Vertical stance (*soo jik sogi*) is a half-facing posture which is useful in either offensive or defensive modes. The knees are straight, the front foot turns inwards 15° from dead ahead, and the rear foot turns 90° to that (**fig. 234**).

Fig. 234

Back fist side strike

We have already encountered back fist which used the large two knuckles in a descending strike to the bridge of the opponent's nose (*dung joomuk taerigi*). This time the strike is made in a horizontal direction to a vertical target such as the opponent's temple (**fig. 235**).

Fig. 235

Fig. 236 Slide your right foot forward and turn your hips away from forward-facing. Bring your right fist back in front of your face and turn it palm-downwards.

Fig. 237 Twist your hips to the front, using this rotational action to help perform back fist. Your fist turns thumb-side up as it strikes the target.

Straight spear finger thrust

The stiffened and extended fingers are used in the form of a spear thrust (*son sonkut tulgi*) to the opponent's vulnerable areas. Form your hand as for knife hand but slightly flex the middle finger to bring it into one line with its two neighbours.

Fig. 238 Step forward with your right foot and bring the left hand over and palm-downwards.

Fig. 239 Flex your left elbow and thrust the right hand over the top, opening the fingers into spear hand. The thumb is uppermost.

110

Fig. 240 Begin to move into left walking stance, folding the right elbow across your chest and drawing back the left hand. Turn your left hand palm-upwards.

Fig. 241 The strike completes as the left hand thrusts forward over the right forearm.

Don't extend the bent guarding arm too far, or it will stick out past your ribs. Also, ensure that the strike is delivered to the mid-line of your body and that it is not too low.

111

Application of part of pattern

The spear thrust described earlier occurs in the pattern *Do San* which is studied later in this syllabus. An opponent seizes hold of your right wrist and you now have to respond (**fig. 242**).

Fig. 242

Fig. 243 Turn your hips away from your partner and thrust the right hand downwards, so his grip is broken.

Fig. 244 Continue turning on your right foot until your back is towards the partner. Bring your left arm up and around.

Fig. 245 Turn completely around, using this rotational energy to help power a back fist side strike to the side of the opponent's head.

Reverse knife hand

Reverse knife hand (*sonkal dung*) uses the area below the index finger-edge to strike the opponent. Form the hand shape as for knife hand but take the thumb further across the palm.

Fig. 246 Stand in left walking stance and swing your right hand around, the palm turning downwards at the moment of impact.

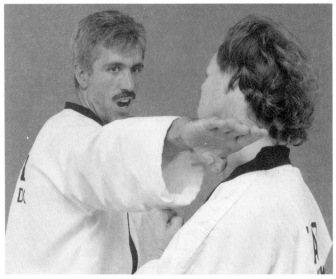

Fig. 247 Use reverse knife hand to attack targets such as the side of the opponent's neck.

Wedging block

Wedging block (*hechyo makgi*) uses a simultaneous thrusting action of both forearms to force the opponent's arms apart.

Fig. 248 Cross your arms in front of your chest, turning the palms of the fists towards you.

Fig. 249 Thrust both arms up and rotate them outwards, blocking the opponent's punches with the little finger-edge of your forearms. CONTINUED

115

Fig. 250 The block is economical and the forearms are taken only to shoulder width.

Fig. 251 The block on the right is too wide. The one on the left has nearly straight elbows. Both are common mistakes to avoid.

Palm block

Palm block (*sonbadak*) uses a similar hand shape to knife hand except that the fingers are more cupped (**fig. 252**). Typically the hand is held with the fingers pointing vertically upwards. Do not allow the hand to tilt forward.

Fig. 252

Fig. 253 *Below, left.* Step back with your right foot and extend the right fist. The left hand is brought palm-outwards in front of your left shoulder.

Fig. 254 *Below.* As the step back is completed, so you must withdraw your right fist to the hip and block across your body with the left hand. The little finger-edge faces away from you.

Turning kick

Turning kick (*dollyo chagi*) uses a pivoting action of the supporting leg to help translate an upwards moving foot into a horizontal arc that strikes the side of the opponent's head or body (**fig. 255**). In this case, the ball of the foot (*ap kumchi*) is used, so the ankle must be flexed 90° and the toes pulled back out of harm's way (**fig. 256**).

Fig. 255   *Left.*

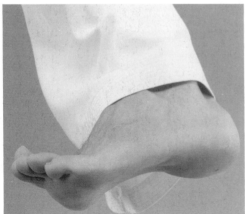

Fig. 256

Fig. 257   Begin from walking stance by turning the lead foot outwards and bringing the rear knee around and up until it points towards the intended target.

Fig. 258   Continue turning on the supporting leg and lean away to counterbalance the weight of your rapidly extending leg. Maintain an effective guard.

Fig. 259   *Above, right.* The kick completes with the body in a 'Y' shape. Keep your head up and your eyes focused on the target.

Fig. 260   Here the knee has simply been raised and not brought around. The kick is said to be 'incorrectly chambered'. CONTINUED

119

Fig. 261 This is another common mistake caused by over-rotating the hips. Recovery from this position is extremely slow, and all the while you are open to attack.

Fig. 262 The heel must be the highest part of the kick, but in this case the little toe is. The heel has dropped because the kick is moving upwards, instead of horizontally.

Side kick

Side kick (*yop chagi*) uses the heel and the little toe-edge of the foot in the configuration known as 'footsword' (*balkal*). Adopt the correct shape by pushing out the heel and raising the toes (**fig. 263**).

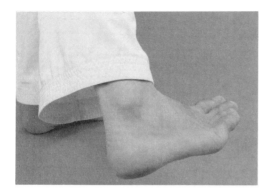

Fig. 263   *Left.*

Fig. 264   *Below, left.* Begin from walking stance by raising your rear knee and bringing it directly forward.

Fig. 265   *Below.* Begin twisting on your supporting leg and continue raising the kicking knee. Allow your shoulders to move naturally so you turn sideways-on to the opponent. CONTINUED

Fig. 266 Begin to thrust your heel out in a straight line to the opponent's mid-section.

Fig. 267 Here the kicking leg is fully extended and the upper body is leaning back to counterbalance it. The heel is the highest part of the kicking foot, and an effective guard is maintained throughout.

Withdraw the kick in the same way it was performed, bringing the foot back to the supporting knee before setting it down once more.

Fig. 268 This is a common mistake of side kick. Lack of hip flexibility has caused the kicking knee to drop so it now points downwards.

Fig. 269 This, too, is a common mistake. The foot shape is incorrect and the flat of the foot is presented to the target. Also, the ball of the foot is higher than the heel.

123

Back kick

Back kick (*dwit chagi*) uses the bottom of the heel in a footsword configuration (*balkal*), but this time the ball of the foot is turned down to the floor (**fig. 270**). The kick is thrust directly out towards an opponent standing behind you (**fig. 271**).

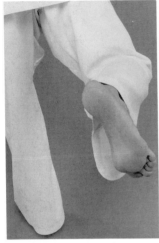

Fig. 270

Fig. 271

124

Fig. 272 Face the opponent in L-stance.

Fig. 273 *Above, right.* Quickly spin around on your leading foot, taking your eyes off the target for the shortest interval of time.

Fig. 274 Keep your elbows close to your sides as you raise the kicking foot and point the heel towards the target.
CONTINUED

Fig. 275 Thrust the heel straight back into the target.

Fig. 276 Pull the spent kick back before dropping it in preparation for turning forward again.

Back kick is a difficult kick to master and there are a number of common mistakes to watch out for.

Fig. 277 The first is caused by turning the upper body too far. It is only necessary to look over your shoulder at the target.

Fig. 278 This shows two common mistakes: the first is that the head is turned away so you cannot see the target; the second is that the arms are splayed out from the body.

Do San

Do San is the pseudonym of Ahn Ch'ang Ho (1876-1938) who devoted his life to furthering the education of Korea and its independence movement. Do San has 24 moves.

Begin from parallel ready stance.

Fig. 279 Turn to the left, step into left walking stance, and perform a high-section outer forearm block.

Fig. 280 Pull back your blocking arm and reverse punch to mid-section.

Fig. 281 Slide your trailing foot across, turn sharply, and perform a second high-section outer forearm block.

Fig. 282 *Above, right.* Pull back your blocking arm and reverse punch to mid-section.

Fig. 283 Slide your left foot across and take up L-stance. At the same time, perform a middle guarding block with knife hand. CONTINUED

Fig. 284 Drop your guard hand palm-downwards and begin to slide your trailing foot forward.

Fig. 285 *Above, right.* Complete the step into right walking stance and thrust right spear hand over the top of your left knuckles.

Fig. 286 The imaginary opponent takes hold of your right wrist and you break his grip by forcing your hand downwards (see again **figs 242–245**).

Fig. 287 Continue turning on your right foot until your back is towards the opponent. Bring your left arm up and around. Extend your right fist palm-downwards across your chest.

Fig. 288 *Above, right.* Turn completely around, using this rotational energy to help power a back fist side strike to the side of the imaginary opponent's head.

Fig. 289 Step forward into right walking stance and perform a second back fist side strike. CONTINUED

131

Fig. 290 Slide your left foot diagonally behind the right and turn into left walking stance. Use the turning energy of the body to help power a high-section outer forearm block.

Fig. 291 *Above, right.* Pull back your blocking arm and reverse punch to mid-section.

Fig. 292 Slide your trailing foot across, turn sharply, and perform another high-section outer forearm block.

Fig. 293 Pull back your blocking arm and reverse punch to mid-section.

Fig. 294 *Below.* Slide your rear foot across and turn sharply through 135° into left walking stance. Perform a wedging block.

Fig. 295 *Below, right.* Keep your shoulders relaxed and your arms steady as you perform front kick to mid-section. CONTINUED

Fig. 296 Drop the spent foot carefully into a right walking stance and perform obverse punch to mid-section.

Fig. 297 Sharply withdraw your right fist and perform reverse punch to mid-section.

Fig. 298 Slide your lead foot across and turn sharply through 90° into right walking stance. Perform a wedging block.

Fig. 299 Keep your shoulders relaxed and your arms steady as you perform front kick to mid-section.

Fig. 300 *Below.* Drop the spent foot carefully into left walking stance and perform obverse punch to mid-section.

Fig. 301 *Below, right.* Sharply withdraw your left fist and perform reverse punch to mid-section. CONTINUED

Fig. 302   Slide your left foot to the left and perform rising block from left walking stance.

Fig. 303   Step forward into right walking stance and perform a second rising block.

Fig. 304 Spin around on your right foot into sitting stance. Perform a horizontal knife strike.

Fig. 305 Bring the left foot to the right, then slide the right foot out into a second sitting stance. Perform a final horizontal knife strike with *kihap*.

Three-step sparring (7)

Go through the preliminaries of bowing and setting the range. The opponent then steps back with his right foot and takes up a low-section outside block. Remain waiting in parallel ready stance.

Fig. 306   Your partner steps forward into right walking stance and performs obverse punch. Step back with your right foot into L-stance and deflect the punch with middle-section outer forearm block.

Fig. 307   The opponent steps into left walking stance and performs the second obverse punch. Respond by stepping back with your left foot and using middle-section outer forearm block.

Fig. 308 The opponent makes his final obverse punch while you step back a good way with your right foot. If you step far enough, then your partner's punch will fall short. Maintain an effective block all the same!

Fig. 309 Bring your right knee forward and perform front kick to the opponent's mid-section.

CONTINUED

139

Fig. 310 Land forward and perform right obverse punch to mid-section.

Fig. 311 Pull back your right fist and reverse punch to mid-section with the left. Don't forget *kihap*.

Three-step sparring (8)

Fig. 312 Your partner steps forward into right walking stance and performs obverse punch. Step back with your right foot into L-stance and deflect the punch with middle-section knife block.

Fig. 313 The opponent steps into left walking stance and performs the second obverse punch. Respond by stepping back with your left foot and using middle-section knife block. CONTINUED

Fig. 314 The opponent makes his final obverse punch while you step back a good way with your right foot. If you step far enough, your partner's punch will fall short.

Fig. 315 Bring your right knee forward and perform side kick to the opponent's mid-section. Use *kihap*.

Fig. 316 *Right.* Land forward in sitting stance and perform right knife hand strike to the opponent's neck. Use a second *kihap* at this point.

Three-step sparring (9)

Fig. 317 Your partner steps forward into right walking stance and performs obverse punch. Step back with your right foot into L-stance and deflect the punch with middle-section inwards palm block.

Fig. 318 The opponent steps into left walking stance and performs the second obverse punch. Respond by stepping back with your left foot and using middle-section inwards palm block.

Fig. 319 The opponent makes his final obverse punch while you pivot on your right foot and slide forward with the left.

Fig. 320 Bring your right knee forward and perform turning kick to the opponent's mid-section. Use *kihap*.

CONTINUED

Fig. 321 Withdraw the spent kicking foot and land in vertical stance (*soo jik sogi*). Perform right knife hand strike to the back of the opponent's neck. Use a second *kihap* at this point.

146

Three-step sparring (10)

Fig. 322   Your partner steps forward
into right walking stance and performs
obverse punch. Step back with your
right foot into L-stance and deflect the
punch with middle-section knife hand
block.   CONTINUED

147

Fig. 323 The opponent steps into left walking stance and performs the second obverse punch. Respond by stepping back with your left foot and using middle-section knife hand block.

Fig. 324 The opponent makes his final obverse punch while you take a good step back with your right foot. Take a sufficiently large step and his punch will fall short.

Fig. 325 Pivot sharply on your left foot and look over your right shoulder.

Fig. 326 Perform back kick to the opponent's mid-section. CONTINUED

Fig. 327 Drop the spent kick to the floor and turn into right walking stance. Use the turning motion to help power a reverse knife hand strike to the side of the opponent's neck.

Semi-free sparring

Semi-free sparring (*ban jayoo matsoki*) is a further development of the three-step sparring we have been practising so far. Until now, the attacker has been limited to using punches, but in semi-free sparring kicks can also be used.

To help introduce you to semi-free sparring, the following three examples have all been prearranged. Later on, you will be able to choose which defence/counter attack to use.

Prearranged sparring is performed on both left and right sides to eliminate bias.

Semi-free sparring (1)

Fig. 328 With a loud *kihap*, the opponent steps into right L-stance. Remain waiting in parallel ready stance.

Fig. 329 The opponent then attacks with right front kick. Step back into right L-stance and deflect the kick with a waist block. CONTINUED

Fig. 330 The opponent performs a second front kick. Step back into left L-stance and perform a second waist block.

Fig. 331 *Below.* The opponent performs a third and final front kick. Step back into right L-stance and block.

Fig. 332 Slide your left foot forward and perform a right reverse punch to mid-section with *kihap*.

Now perform this sequence on the other side.

Semi-free sparring (2)

Fig. 333 With a loud *kihap*, the opponent steps into right L-stance. Remain waiting in parallel ready stance. The opponent then attacks with right turning kick. Step back into right L-stance and deflect the kick with waist block.

Fig. 334 The opponent performs a second turning kick. Step back into left L-stance and perform a waist block.

Fig. 335 The opponent performs a third and final turning kick. Step back into right L-stance and block.

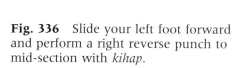

Fig. 336 Slide your left foot forward and perform a right reverse punch to mid-section with *kihap*.

Now perform this sequence on the other side.

155

Semi-free sparring (3)

Fig. 337 With a loud *kihap*, the opponent steps into right L-stance. Remain waiting in parallel ready stance. The opponent then attacks with right side kick. Step back into right L-stance and deflect the kick with a waist block.

Fig. 338 The opponent performs a second side kick. Step back into left L-stance and perform a waist block.

Fig. 339 The opponent performs a third and final side kick. Step back into right L-stance and block.

Fig. 340 Slide your left foot forward and perform a right reverse punch to mid-section with *kihap*.

Now repeat this sequence on the other side.

Appendix
Korean terminology

Tae kwon-do is a Korean martial art, so Korean terminology is used. Learning this means you will be able to train all over the world and understand what is being asked of you.

About turn   *Dwiyro torro*
Attention!   *Charyot*
Attention stance   *Charyot sogi*

Back fist   *Dung joomuk*
Back fist strike   *Dung joomuk taerigi*
Back kick   *Dwit chagi*
Backwards   *Dwiyro kaggi*
Ball of foot   *Ap kumchi*
Begin   *Si jak*
Belt   *Ti*
Bow   *Kyong Ye*

Dismiss   *Haessan*

Eight   *Yodoll*

Fingertips   *Sonkut*
Five   *Dasaul*
Footsword   *Balkal*
Forearm   *Palmok*
Forefist   *Ap joomuk*
Forward   *Apro kaggi*
Four   *Neth*
Four-directional punch   *Sajo jirugi*
Front kick   *Ap chagi*
Front rising kick   *Apcha olligi*

Guarding block   *Daebi makgi*

Heel   *Dwikumchi*
High-section   *Nopunde*

Inner forearm   *An palmok*
Inner forearm block   *An palmok makgi*
Instructor   *Sabum*
Inward   *Anaero*

Kick   *Chagi*
Knife hand   *Sonkal*
Knife hand guarding block   *Sonkal daebi makgi*
Knife hand strike   *Sonkal taerigi*

L-stance   *Niunja sogi*
Left   *Wen*
Low-section   *Najunde*

Middle-section   *Kaunde*

Nine   *Ahop*

Obverse punch   *Baro jirugi*
One   *Hanna*
Outer forearm   *Bakat palmok*
Outer forearm block   *Bakat palmok makgi*
Outward   *Bakaero*

Palm   *Sonbadak*
Parallel stance   *Narani sogi*
Pattern   *Tul*

Ready   *Chunbi*
Return to ready stance   *Barrol*
Reverse punch   *Bandae jirugi*
Right   *Orun*
Rising block   *Chookyo makgi*

Semi-free sparring   *Ban jayoo matsoki*
Seven   *Ilgop*
Shout   *Kihap*
Side kick   *Yop chagi*
Side rising kick   *Yopcha olligi*
Sitting stance   *Annun sogi*
Six   *Yosaul*
Sparring   *Matsoki*
Spear thrust   *Sonkut tulgi*
Stop   *Goman*
Straight   *Son*
Student   *Jeja*

Ten   *Yoll*
Three   *Seth*
Three-step sparring   *Sambo matsoki*
Thrust   *Tulgi*
Training hall   *Dojang*
Training uniform   *Dobok*
Turning kick   *Dollyo chagi*
Twin forearm block   *Sang palmok makgi*
Two   *Dool*

Vertical stance   *Soo jik sogi*

Waist block   *Hori makgi*
Walking stance   *Gunnun sogi*
Wedging block   *Hechyo makgi*

X-stance   *Kyocha sogi*

Index